Hospital Heroe

by Rashmi Sirdeshpande
Illustrated by Patrick Corrigan

Contents

OXFORD
UNIVERSITY PRESS

Meet Shaku!

Shaku

Shaku is a surgeon. Surgeons try to find out what is wrong with patients. They also do all kinds of operations to help their patients feel better.

Surgeons like Shaku do not do everything on their own. They work with a large team of nurses, doctors and other hospital staff. Let's meet some of them.

The children's ward

Shaku goes to the children's **ward**. She gets the notes about a new patient called Noah. Noah needs a small operation to remove his appendix.

Your appendix is like a little pouch inside you.

appendix

Noah's appendix is sore, and it is making his tummy hurt.

Shaku goes to see Noah. Today, she is wearing a hat which has dinosaurs on it. Noah loves dinosaurs and the hat makes him smile.
Noah has his own hospital bed, and there are lovely pictures on the wall. There are chairs next to the bed for Noah's mum and dad.

Talking about the operation

Sue, the nurse, is with Noah. Shaku asks Noah how he is feeling. She talks to Noah and his mum and dad about the operation, and answers all their questions.

Is there anything else you'd like to know, Noah?

Shaku has to get her patient's permission before any operation. As Noah is a child, his mum or dad will do this for him.

Then, Shaku needs to go and get ready to do the operation. Noah will wait in the children's ward until it is time to go to the **operating theatre**.

The huddle

Before the operation, the whole team gets together to plan what they will do and what they will need. This team meeting is called a huddle.

The anaesthetist (*say*: an-<u>ees</u>-thet-ist) uses a special medicine called *anaesthetic* (*say*: an-es-<u>thet</u>-ic) to help Noah fall asleep. This will stop him feeling any pain during the operation.

The **registrar** helping Shaku is a trainee surgeon.

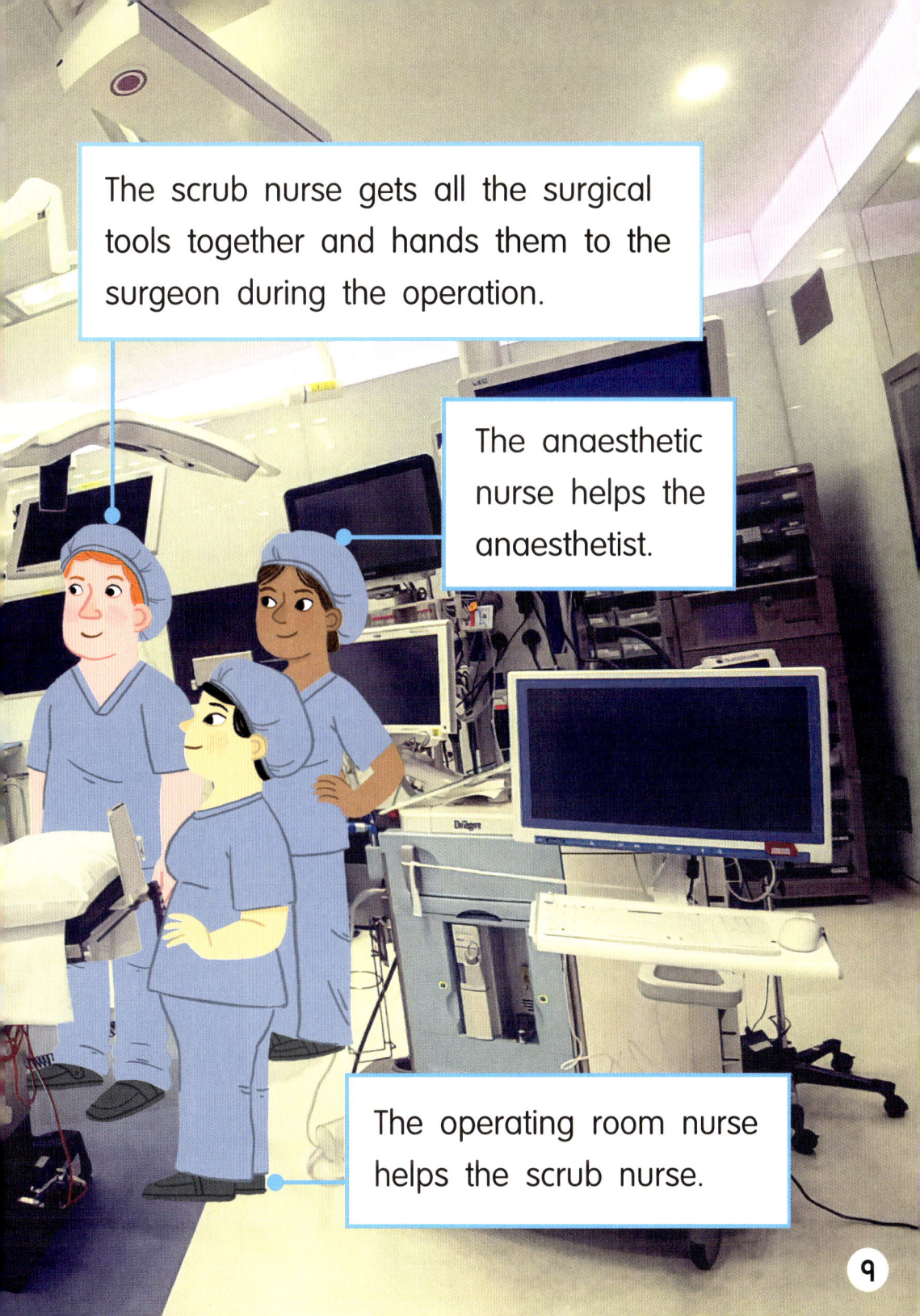

The scrub nurse gets all the surgical tools together and hands them to the surgeon during the operation.

The anaesthetic nurse helps the anaesthetist.

The operating room nurse helps the scrub nurse.

Bringing in the patient

When they are all set, the operating team calls for the patient to be brought in. The porter, Jim, will bring Noah to the anaesthetic room.

Jim is cheerful and friendly. He makes sure Noah is comfortable and relaxed.

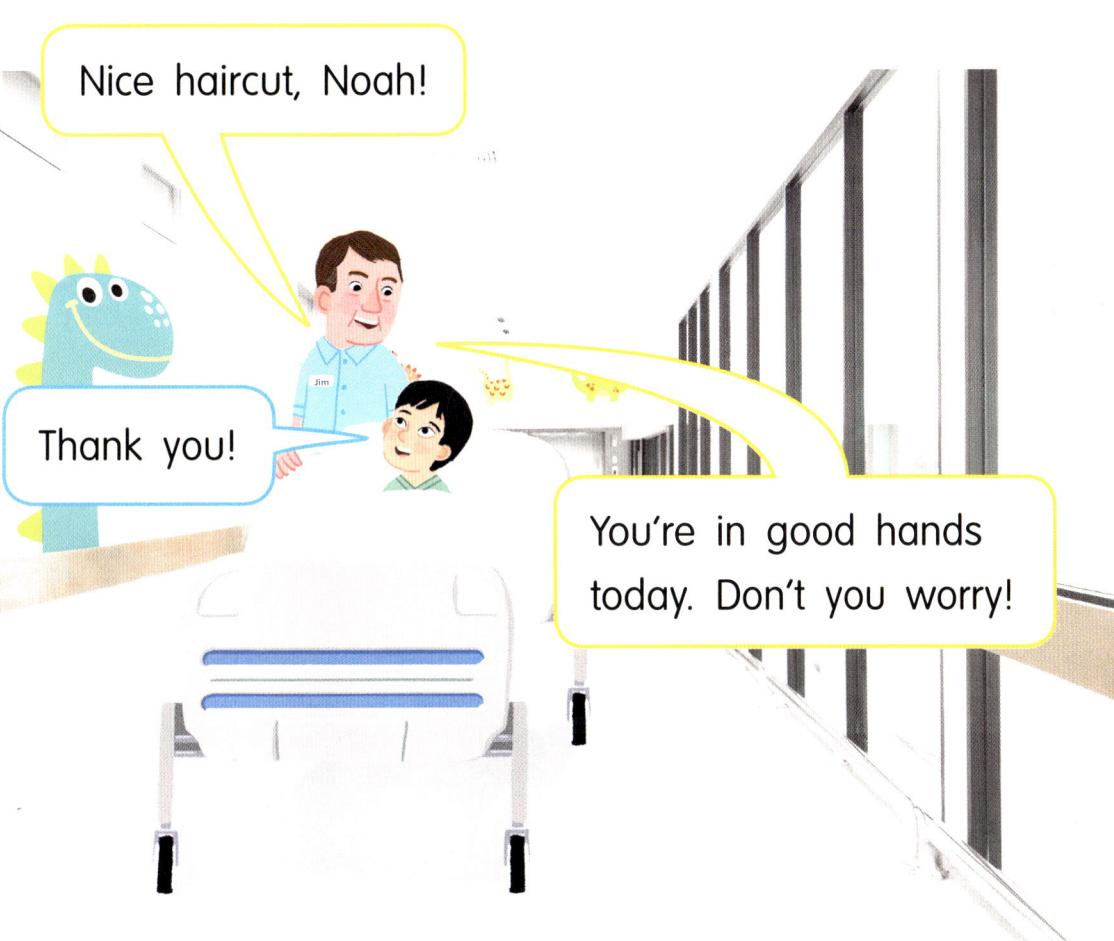

Nice haircut, Noah!

Thank you!

You're in good hands today. Don't you worry!

Jim does not just move people around the hospital. After dropping Noah off, Jim will help move some important equipment.

The anaesthetic room

The anaesthetic nurse does some safety checks to make sure they have the right patient. Then the anaesthetist will use some anaesthetic to help Noah fall asleep.

Some types of anaesthetic just take away the feeling of pain while the patient stays awake. With general anaesthetic, the patient goes to sleep and will not notice anything at all.

The general anaesthetic works fast. Noah is off to sleep in just a few seconds.

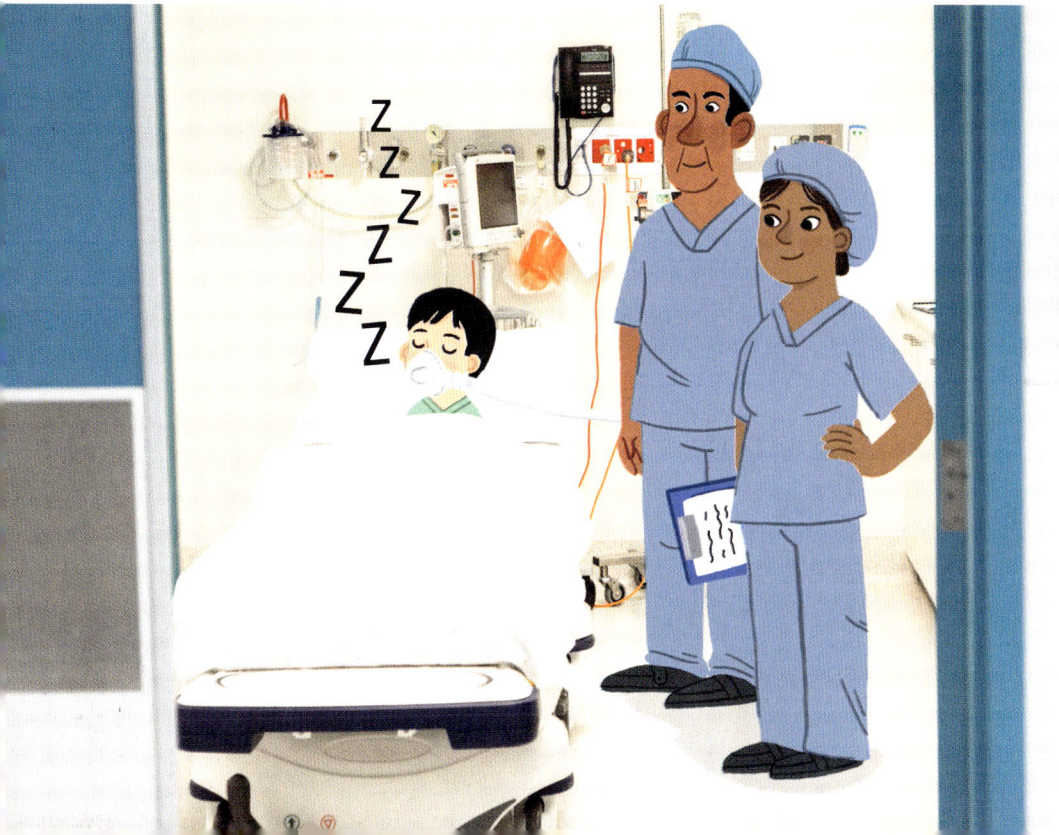

The operating theatre

Meanwhile, in the operating theatre, the team is getting ready for the operation. Everyone in the team has washed their hands and is wearing special clothes called scrubs.

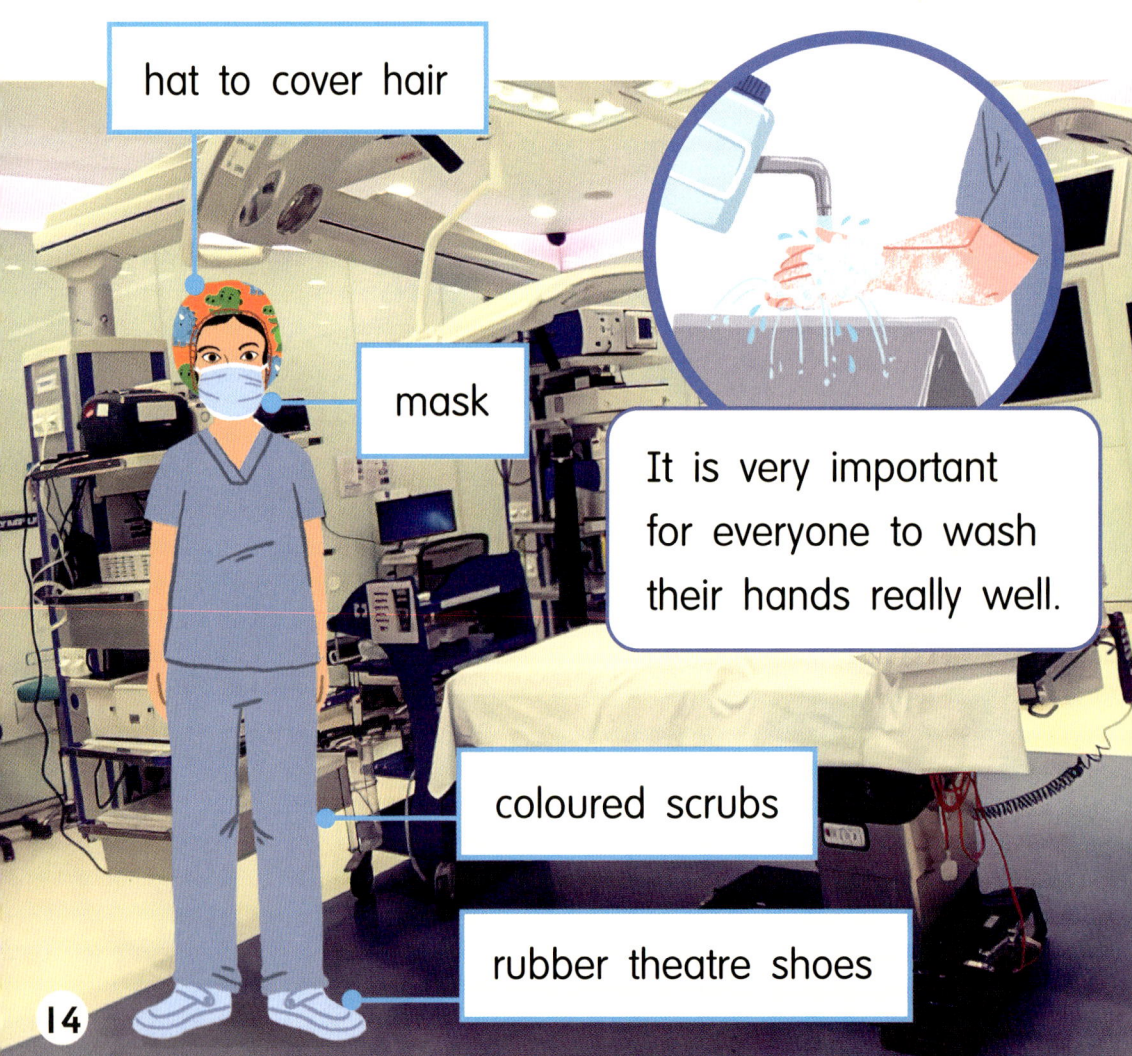

hat to cover hair

mask

It is very important for everyone to wash their hands really well.

coloured scrubs

rubber theatre shoes

The scrub nurse checks that all the equipment is working and that the tools are all **sterile**. This is really important because dirty tools could make Noah ill.

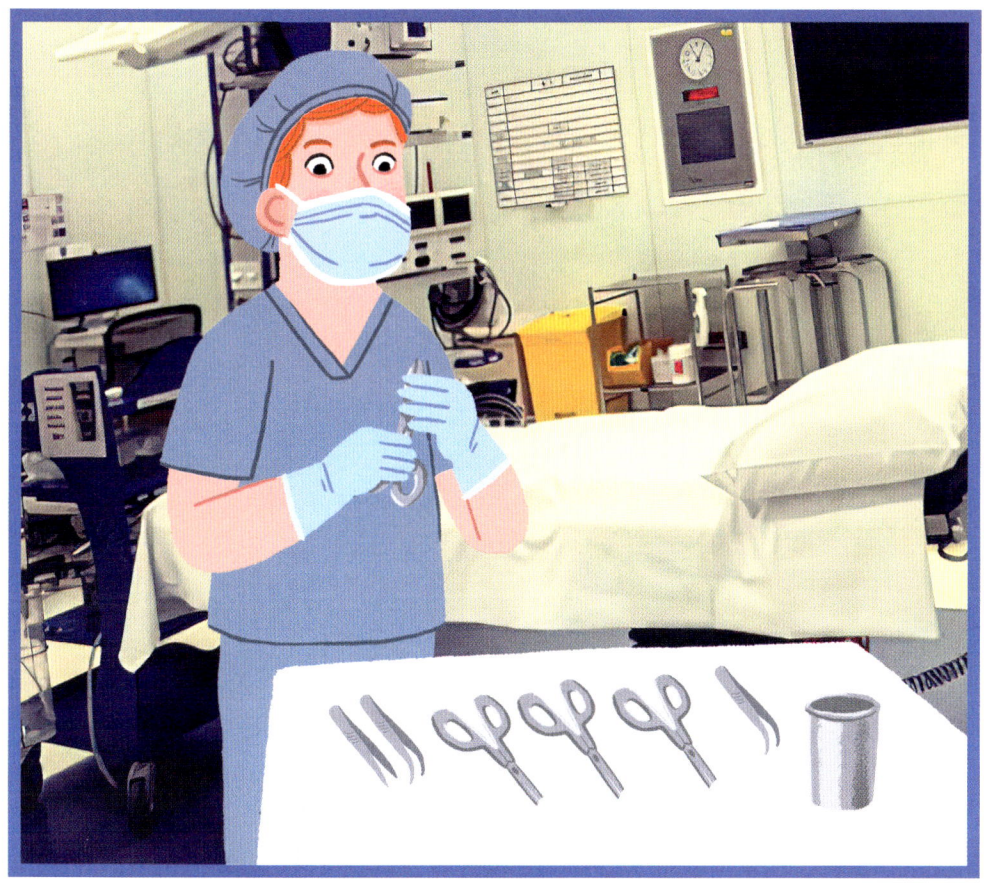

When everything is ready, Noah is brought into the operating room.

The operation

Just before the operation, there is a 'time out'. One last time, the team checks that this is the correct patient and the right operation.

Once the operation begins, everyone needs to focus and work together.

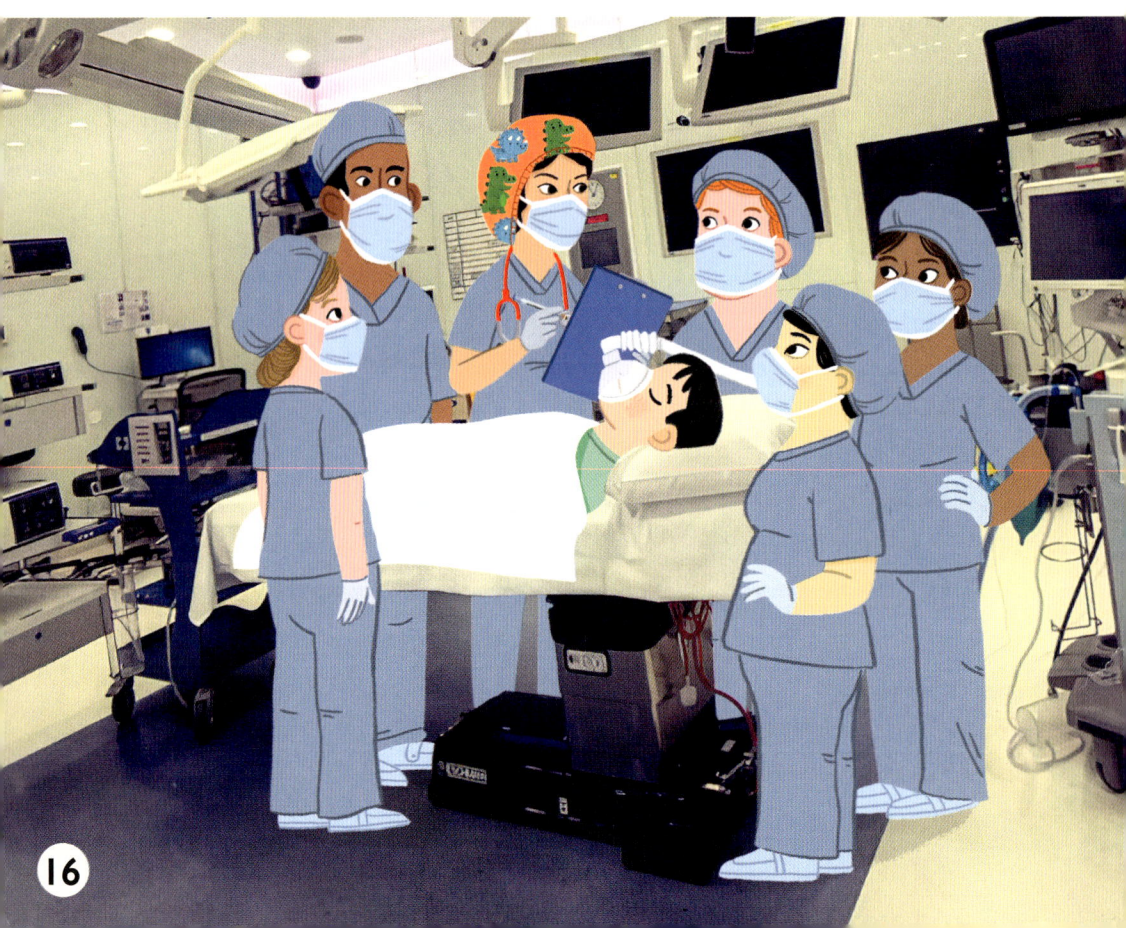

During an operation, surgeons ask scrub nurses to pass them their tools.

Stefan has been a nurse for many years. Before Shaku even asks for a tool, he has already passed it to her. When teams know each other really well, they know exactly what to do and when to do it.

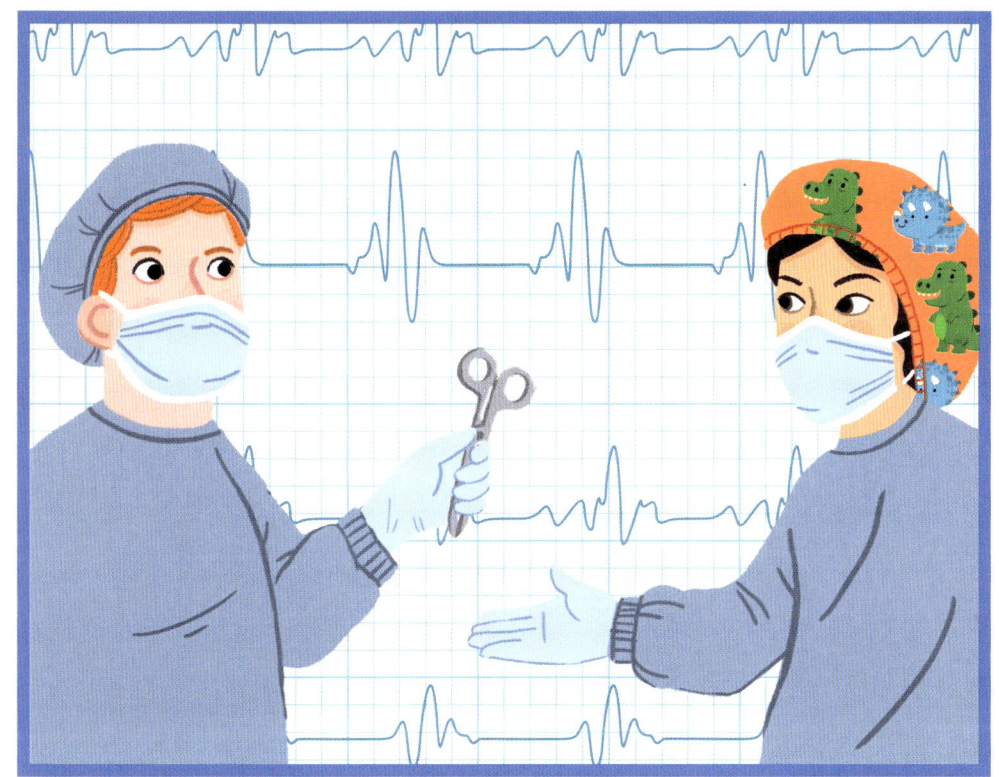

After the operation

Noah's operation was a success! Afterwards, Noah is sent to the recovery ward. This is where he will stay until the anaesthetic wears off and he wakes up. Sue, the nurse, is here to look after him.

Noah is in the recovery ward.

Meanwhile, the operating team talk about how things went. They take notes on what happened. Then it is time to get the room ready for the next operation.

Surgeons often do lots of operations in a day.

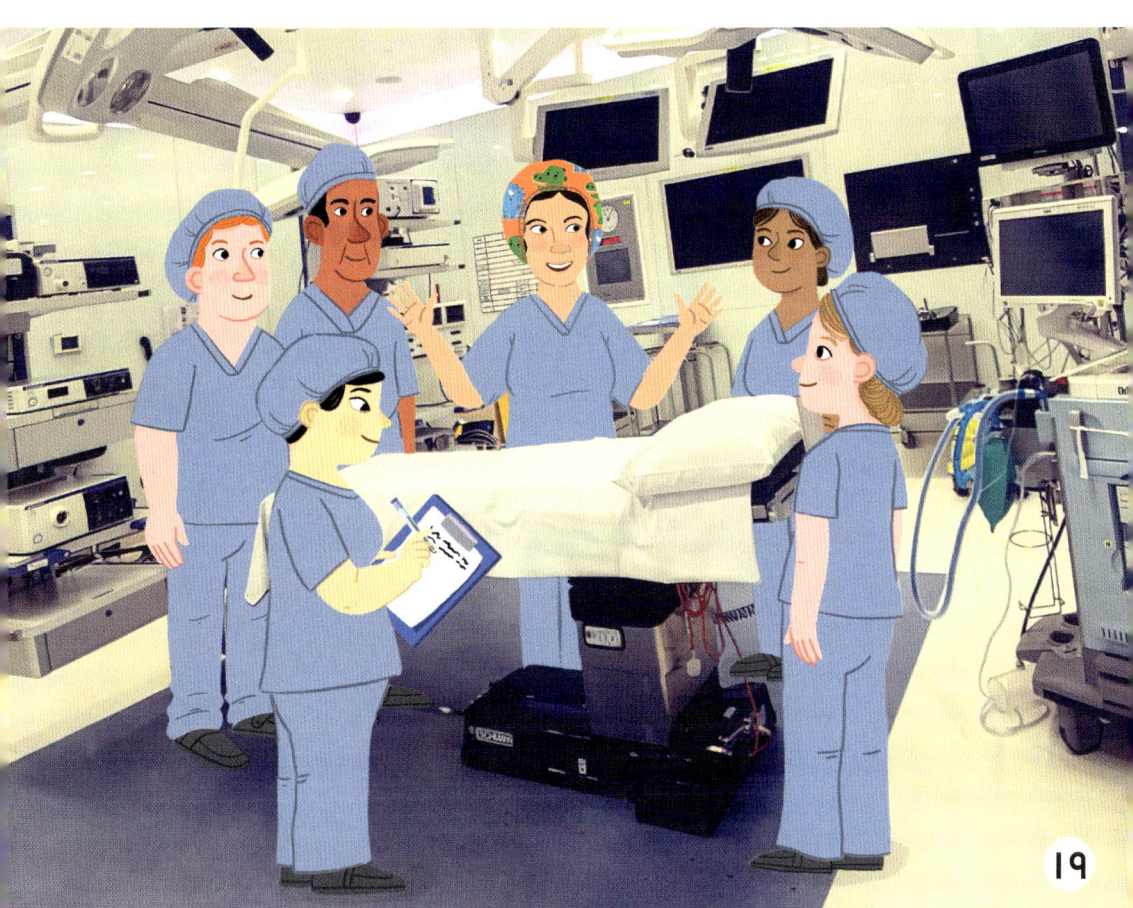

Recovery time

Noah slowly wakes up. He feels a bit sleepy, but he is OK. The medicine stops him from feeling any pain. Noah's family have come to the recovery ward to see him. They are proud of him for being so brave.

Shaku comes back to check on Noah.
She speaks to Sue to see how he has
been doing.

How are you
feeling now, Noah?

After a few hours, when Noah is feeling
much better, he is taken back to the
children's ward.

Home time

The next morning, Noah has some toast with butter. Shaku checks on Noah again. When she is sure that he is well enough, he is ready to be sent home.
She tells Noah and his family what to expect over the next few weeks.

Your tummy might be sore for a few days but you will be OK. Make sure you get lots of rest!

Noah's family collect some medicines to help with his pain. They leave a thank-you note and a big box of chocolates for all the hospital team, then off they go!

Noah and his family leave a gift to say thank you for looking after him.

Thank you

Glossary

operating theatre: a room in a hospital where operations are done

registrar: a doctor who is learning new skills so they can work in a special role in a hospital

sterile: completely clean

ward: a room in a hospital

Index